The Strange World of Elijah and Elisha

Helen Paynter

Director of the Centre for the

Study of Bible and Violence, Bristol Baptist College

GROVE BOOKS LIMITED

RIDLEY HALL RD CAMBRIDGE CB3 9HU

Contents

Acknowledgments

This booklet represents a portion of my doctoral work, conducted at Bristol Baptist College between 2011 and 2015 under the supervision of the Revd Dr Peter Hatton and the Revd Dr Knut Heim. I am deeply indebted to them for their wise counsel, and also to the college for its superb support, encouragement and library service. It is my privilege still to be part of this worshipping, studying community and to work with colleagues who are friends. As always, I am grateful to my husband Stephen and my daughters Susanna, Louisa and Victoria for their unwavering love and support.

First Impression December 2019
ISSN 1365-490X
ISBN 978 1 78827 105 9

Introduction

1

A prominent social commentator is wanted by the leader of an enemy nation because of the stories he has been publishing, so the leader sends a raiding party to abduct him. When the soldiers have the social commentator cornered, they are all inexplicably struck blind. In their confusion a voice offers to lead them to the man they are looking for, so they follow him without demur. Suddenly, their blindness lifts, and they discover that they have been led into the capital city of the enemy nation. And there is its king, and there is the social commentator—he was the one they had been following all along! For a minute the king looks as if he might kill them all, but the social commentator pleads on their behalf. So the king throws them a banquet and they all go home, well fed, agreeably drunk, but without the man they came for.

The story is odd—burlesque, even—and you probably recognized that if you substitute the prophet Elisha for 'social commentator,' it is straight out of 2 Kings 6. But what is the function of such a story in our sacred text? Is it possible that it is intended to be humorous? And if so, why?

In my own thinking on the Elijah and Elisha stories I began with this story and these questions, and found that it led into a project that uncovered a complex and sophisticated use of two major literary devices within the central portion of Kings (1 Kings 17–2 Kings 13).[1] These devices are *carnivalization* and *mirroring*. Both will be described more fully in chapters that follow, but a brief definition is in order here. *Carnivalization* is the existence within literature of humorous features typically seen in medieval carnival. Such features include inversion, ribaldry, unusual speech patterns, and mockery, and we will look at these later. *Mirroring* is the presence within a literary text of two narratives or characters which seem to share many features and thus mirror one another. Mirroring is a device whereby the author can offer internal commentary on a character or sequence of events.

Before we can proceed, let me make some preliminary comments about the Book of Kings. The first is to explain my use of this term in the singular. The reason that we have 1 Kings and 2 Kings is simply a function of the size of a scroll in the ancient world. The combined book is too large to fit into a single document, and so was divided. However, it is intended to be read through, and without break. For this reason it should be treated as a literary whole; themes, ideas and literary devices span the break. Treating the document as two separate books can make it extremely difficult for us to detect subtle repetitions and allusions that occur between the two halves.

The Book of Kings is largely a sober and sobering account of the gradual degeneracy of the monarchy in both Israel (the northern kingdom) and Judah (in the south). Once the reign of Solomon has been described, it largely falls into a formulaic repetition of the evaluation of each king's reign: how long he lived; how good or bad he was; who succeeded him; and where he was buried.

But into the middle of this depressing and sometimes—to us—dull chronicle, the stories of Elijah and Elisha, along with the stories of the nation of Aram (Syria in some translations), burst like a minor explosion. Elijah and Elisha are anything but dull; they are active, vibrant, bad-tempered, do a wide range of miracles and frankly sometimes act bizarrely.

This interjection raises some questions which traditional understandings of the Book of Kings generally fail to answer. They are as follows.

Were the Prophets Righteous?

Elijah and Elisha have traditionally been held up as heroes of faith; many devout believers assume that their actions are righteous by definition. But a frank consideration of some of their actions may make us uncomfortable. So, for example, in 2 Kings 1, Elijah calls down fire to consume 102 men, apparently on a whim; in 2 Kings 8, Elisha appears to send a false prophecy to Ben-Hadad and to incite Hazael to his murder; and perhaps most strikingly of all, in 2 Kings 2, Elisha summons two bears to 'rip to pieces' 42 youths who have mocked him. Such stories might lead us to ask the question of whether we really ought to approve of everything that a prophet of God does.

Why is Elijah Commanded to Anoint Elisha, Hazael and Jehu?

In 1 Kgs 19.15–17, God gives an unexpected instruction to Elijah, which raises several questions:

> You shall anoint Hazael to be king over Aram. And Jehu the son of Nimshi you shall anoint to be king over Israel, and Elisha the son of Shaphat of Abel-meholah you shall anoint to be prophet in your place. And the one who escapes from the sword of Hazael shall Jehu put to death, and the one who escapes from the sword of Jehu shall Elisha put to death (1 Kgs 19.15–17).[2]

Why is Elijah, prophet of the LORD in Israel, charged with appointing a king of Aram? Such interference in the internal affairs of a pagan nation is unprecedented in the Hebrew Bible. And these verses name individuals who will not appear for years within the narrative, or chapters, within the text. Why are they identified at this point in the story?

The Prominence of Israel and Aram

The main theological priority of the Book of Kings concerns Judah and the reason for her exile. But the Elijah / Elisha narratives and the stories of Aram are mainly set within Israel, and many of them contain no reference to Judah at all. This is puzzling; if the text receives its final editing during or after the Judean exile, long after Israel has ceased to be an entity, why Israel's prominence in this portion of the book?

We might be even more surprised by the prominence of Aram, and the positive way in which this pagan nation is often viewed. So, for example, its king requests—and obtains—favours for a senior army officer (2 Kings 5). The king of Israel throws a banquet for an Aramean raiding party (2 Kings 6). And Elisha appears to enjoy a privileged status in the court of Aram, culminating in the unofficial appointing of their new dynastic line (2 Kings 8).

Light is shed on these unanswered questions if we read the central section of Kings with attention to the possibility of humour in the text. As we shall see, identifying the literary carnivalization and mirroring uncovers a seditious critique of prophets, kings and even Judah herself.

2 Carnivalization of Literature

In the mid-twentieth century the Russian literary theorist Mikhail Bakhtin published his doctoral dissertation in a book entitled *Rabelais and His World*.[3] In it he explored the phenomenon of carnival, and how it permeates literature. While we might rightly associate carnival in its fullest and most florid form with the High Middle Ages, Bakhtin traced its roots back as far as the Roman Saturnalia, and claimed that the ritualized use of pageantry and laughter can be identified in most cultures since.

Medieval carnival was characterized by feasts, fairs, clowns, fools, jugglers, performing animals and what might be termed a pageantry of inversion. During the feast, normal hierarchies and social barriers were suspended or inverted; sacred ritual was mocked and parodied; the grotesque was celebrated; the normal laws of the land were replaced by carnival rule; and scatological (toilet) humour abounded. Obscenities, curses and billingsgate replaced normal verbal etiquette.[4] The beggar became a king (and the king a beggar); fasting was replaced by feasting; the profane parodied the sacred. Emphasis was placed upon bodily orifices, particularly the genitalia, which represent the twin concepts of decay (excrement) and procreation. Another key feature of carnival was the juxtaposition of opposites. The sacred mingled with the profane, the lofty with the low, the wise with the foolish. Hierarchies were not simply inverted but subverted, in what Bakhtin described as 'joyful relativity.'[5] Those who mocked became the mocked themselves. The carnival king and boy bishop were dethroned with abuse. Carnival was normal life inside out, back to front and upside down.

Carnival was normal life inside out, back to front and upside down

Bakhtin's particular contribution was to describe how these features of carnival behaviour find their way into literature. Although he considered that it was present in its highest form in sixteenth century CE literature, he also found it in various other periods, extending back as far as Greek writers in the third century BCE.

In carnivalized literature, certainty is turned into ambiguity, normally polar opposites are juxtaposed, and official forms of language and rhetoric are transgressed. The monologue of the dominant voice of the powerful is not replaced with a monologue of the peasant, but rather replaced with a multitude of voices which leave a text that is rich, ambivalent and open-ended.

Using the work of Bakhtin and others who have developed his ideas further, a set of distinctive features of carnivalized literature can be formulated.[6] These can be represented in six categories:

- Unusual use of language: foreign-sounding speech, cursing, vulgarity, abusive speech;
- Inversion of hierarchies: the making and unmaking of temporary 'monarchs;'
- Foolery: the seeming simpleton who speaks truth to power;
- Feasting: unusual, unexpected feasts;
- Unusual expression of things that are vulgar, grotesque or offensive;
- Bizarre, unexpected breaches of normal cause and consequence.

Is it plausible that we might find such comedic writing within our sacred text? Many have considered that this is highly unlikely, following two different lines of reasoning. First, some consider that there is an ethical incompatibility between humour and the serious nature of Scripture. Certainly, if humour amounts to frivolity, and is incompatible with the serious pursuit of truth, then we should not expect to find it in the Bible, which clearly speaks of serious and important matters.

However, humour is not incompatible with serious purpose. Writing in the nineteenth century, William Hazlitt argued that ridicule can have a positive ethical purpose—indeed, may be a *truth-seeking* device.

> Ridicule is the test of truth...it does not contain or attempt a formal proof of it, but owes its power of conviction to the bare suggestion of it...[7]

More modern authors such as Ronald de Sousa agree. 'Laughter is revelatory of the nature of reality.'[8] Bakhtin himself considered that carnivalesque literature was peculiarly suited to testing ultimate questions. We see the use of satirical humour in the protest of many modern resistance organizations, including those operating in places where outright dissent would be quickly suppressed. Far from precluding a serious investigation of truth, I would argue that humour might sometimes provide the *only vehicle* for demonstrating subversive or dangerous truths.

The second reason why some people argue that we cannot plausibly identify humour in the Old Testament is that they consider ancient patterns of humour to be necessarily inaccessible to a modern audience, since it was written in a different language and within an ancient, premodern culture.

It is true that many years of reading these texts seriously, either as devout readers in the pew, or as heavyweight scholars seeking to analyze them critically, have conditioned many of us to view them as serious, solemn documents and nothing else. And naturally our limited understanding of the original language of composition of the texts will restrict our ability to discern humour within them, even for those who are expert in Hebrew and Aramaic. We are also much less likely to detect 'in' jokes or humour that has a very specific cultural referent. Humour relating to our own political predicament will be hard to understand several thousand years from now.

> **Humour within biblical narrative often lies at the level of events, rather than wordplay**

Nonetheless, there are some factors which make the detection of humour more plausible than we might think. Humour within biblical narrative often lies at the level of events, rather than in close wordplay—though wordplay may also be a feature, and we do detect this. Additionally Melissa Jackson, who has written on the presence of humour within the Bible, argues that repeated attentive reading sensitizes us to its comedic elements.[9] We gain competence in detecting humour as we grow in experience.

For example, on repeated hearing or reading, the Naboth story (1 Kings 21) reveals a wordplay between the description of Ahab as sullen and ill-humoured, and the stubborn and rebellious son of Deut 21.18–19. This is one of several points of similarity between the two texts, leading the attentive hearer to the ironical conclusion that Naboth, a paradigm of filial responsibility, receives the fate due to the disobedient son, while the 'sullen' Ahab benefits from his death (1 Kgs 21.3).[10]

Such repeated readings, or hearings, appear to have been standard for the way in which the text was originally used, and increase the plausibility of subtle humorous nuance being present, detectable only upon deep and prolonged repetition.[11]

If, as I have argued above, humour is sometimes the only means of expressing dangerous political truth, then we might *expect* there to be comedic elements within Scripture. James Scott describes how situations of power imbalance always result in both an 'official' conversation and a 'hidden' transcript, by which means the poor are able to express their frustration and contempt without being held up to the charge of insubordination.[12] Working with Scripture itself, Yairah Amit has identified 'hidden polemics,' places where the reader is left with a particular impression after reading the text, but where the author has attempted both to conceal the subject of the polemic and yet at the same time to leave traces of it.[13] For example, there are numerous subtle allusions to Saul in the story of the Levite's wife (Judges 19), which Amit argues amount to a concealed critique of his kingship.

And what of carnivalization itself? Is it plausible that this genre of writing which Bakhtin traces back as far as the third century BCE but no further, might be found within Scripture? In fact, carnival crops up in many cultures, ancient and modern. Carnival-like behaviour is found in the ancient Near-East. For example, the Babylonian new moon festival includes the ritual striking of the king, which amounts to a decrowning event as described by Bakhtin. Within literature, carnivalization has been detected in writings from cultures quite unconnected to the Greco-Roman world—in Far Eastern writing, for example. There is reasonable evidence that carnivalization is a near-universal form of expression, which commonly emerges in the face of power structures unassailable by conventional means.

In recent years, there has been a growing interest within the world of biblical studies into the work of Mikhail Bakhtin, and the possibility that it might provide a useful insight into biblical texts. As a result, carnivalesque elements have been detected in Esther, Ruth, Daniel and Kings.[14]

Building upon the work of humour theorists Melissa Jackson and Paul Lauter, I consider that the evidence for the carnivalization of a biblical text can be regarded as summing up to 'proof' when four conditions are satisfied.[15] First, the distinctive features are present, and in clusters, not sporadically; secondly, the new interpretation which arises can help account for some otherwise inexplicable problems within the text; thirdly, the new interpretation should demonstrate coherence with the wider text in terms of effect; and fourthly, it should be supported by the findings of other scholars.

We will now consider whether these conditions are satisfied when the lens is applied to the Book of Kings.

3 Carnivalization in Kings?

In the previous chapter I identified six distinctive features of carnivalesque writing. An analysis of the whole of Kings for these features reveals that while most parts contain the odd instance, in the central section (1 Kings 13 to 2 Kings 10) there is an enormous number of them. One of the test criteria is that the distinctive features should be present in clusters, so it is upon this central section that we will now focus. We will consider the distinctive features one at a time.

Unusual Use of Language: Foreign-Sounding Speech, Cursing, Vulgarity, Abusive Speech

The central section of Kings has many linguistic anomalies, and they fall into two main categories. First, there are many occurrences of abnormal linguistic forms of Hebrew. The origin of these is disputed, but they may well represent non-standard, colloquial Hebrew as used in Israel (rather than Judah). These colloquialisms cluster within direct speech more than within the narration around it, suggesting that there is a deliberate foreignization of some of the characters by the writer—in much the same way that a modern writer from the south of England might make a character in her book speak with a Glaswegian or Yorkshire accent.

The second type of linguistic transgression is 'billingsgate'—curses, oaths, insults and other such coarse speech. Once again, the central section of Kings has many florid examples. There is mockery (1 Kgs 18.27; 22.24; 2 Kgs 2.23); insult (1 Kgs 18.17; 20.10; 21.20; 2 Kgs 2.23; 9.34); physical violence (1 Kgs 22.24); sarcasm (1 Kgs 18.27); sexual innuendo (1 Kgs 21.21; 2 Kgs 9.22) and sheer insolence (1 Kgs 21.20; 22.16; 2 Kgs 3.13,14). There are references to unclean dogs and their defilement of corpses; to sexual promiscuity; to urination and perhaps even, elliptically, to castration and defecation. A few examples are given here.

- 1 Kgs 18.27: *Call in a louder voice, for he is a god! Perhaps he is meditating; perhaps he has withdrawn to the side; perhaps he is on a journey; perhaps he is asleep and must be woken.* Elijah's mocking words to the prophets of Baal imply that their god might be defecating, which is the probable inference from 'He has withdrawn to the side.'

- 1 Kgs 21.21: *I am bringing disaster upon you. And I will consume and after you I will cut off to Ahab the one that pisses against a wall.* Here Elijah, again speaking to the king, this time in God's name, uses vulgar language to indicate that every male in the king's line will be killed. But is this, at the same time, a reference to the cutting off of the male member of each of the male (family) members?
- 1 Kgs 21.24: *The dogs will eat Jezebel within the ramparts of Jezreel. The dead of Ahab within the city, the dogs will eat, and the dead in the field, the birds of the sky will eat.* Continuing in the same insulting vein, the prophet invokes unclean dogs and the (to the ancient mind) drastic theme of non-burial to describe Jezebel's fate.
- 2 Kgs 9.22: *[Jehu to Joram] What peace? As long as the whoring of Jezebel your mother and her many sorceries continue?* There is no suggestion within the narrative that Jezebel was sexually unfaithful to Ahab, but Jehu slurs her virtue nonetheless.

Inversion of Hierarchies: the Making and Unmaking of Temporary 'Kings' and 'Queens'

The theme of inversion can be identified when an individual experiences reversal of status, but also when they show attributes which are the opposite of what one might expect. (Bakhtin speaks of themes such as the virtuous courtesan or the generous bandit.) Again, there are many examples within the central section of Kings—see in particular 1 Kings 20, 2 Kgs 5; 6.8–7.20; 9.1–10.27.

In 2 Kings 5, the great warrior Naaman, described in superlative terms in verse 1, has to be instructed by the 'little lass' who serves his wife (v 2). He must then humble himself to submit to the instructions of Elisha, bathing in the Jordan seven times. And when he emerges from the water, his skin is like that of a 'lad' (v 14), the masculine version of the same word used to describe the serving girl.

Wordplay in 2 Kings 7 emphasizes the satirical purpose of the narrator, describing the dramatic overthrow of the siege of Samaria. The scornful officer who disbelieves the promise of deliverance (v 2) suggests that rescue might come through divine 'windows' (*arubot*). Rather, it comes through just four (*arbah*) men (v 3). In fact, they are lepers (*mizra'im*), but the Arameans think they are fleeing from Egyptians (*mizraim*). Of course, lepers were excluded from military service, intensifying the irony.

Perhaps the most florid examples of unexpected reversal occur when Ahab and Jezebel meet their end in 1 Kings 22 and 2 Kings 9. Ahab's death is not simply told, but described as a great downfall. First dressed in his royal finery (1 Kings 22.10), he lays this aside (v 30), ending up slumped in his chariot, the dogs lapping up his blood (v 34). And Jezebel's downfall is quite literal. Her physical and social elevation (in 22.31 she is upstairs, she does her hair, applies cosmetics and speaks pridefully) serves to maximize the effect of her ignominious death, where these states are abruptly reversed and she is thrown out of the window by her own men (v 33). Again, the dogs are at work, not simply lapping her blood, but consuming almost her entire body (v 35).

The fool is a familiar literary figure who speaks truth to power. By refusing to comply with normal convention, he uncovers the folly of his masters. We have already briefly considered the four lepers of 2 Kings 7, who function in this way.

The prophet Micaiah (1 Kings 22) is brought into an impressive courtroom, with the court prophets charging about in a frenzy predicting military success before the grandly-arrayed kings of Israel and Judah (vv 10–11). Micaiah does not mimic their prophetic ecstasy and refuses to collude with their lies, using the prophets' own words in sarcastic parody (v 15).

The disguised prophet of 1 Kgs 20.35–43 uses a similar means of speaking truth to power. He seeks injury to his own person, allowing him to approach the king in disguise, and giving him a means of entrapping the king with his own words.

According to Bakhtin, foolery is often associated with disguise and deception, as here. Indeed, we see disguise and deception in multiple places within our text. We have the king of Israel disguising himself as a commoner while the king of Judah wears his royal finery into battle (1 Kgs 22.30); an unfulfilled prophecy (2 Kgs 3.19, compare v 27); visual and auditory trickery (2 Kgs 3.22–23; 7.6); Elisha urging Hazael to lie to his master (2 Kgs 8.10); and blatant deception by Jehu in 2 Kgs 10.18.

Feasting: Unusual, Unexpected Feasts

In contrast with the formal and hierarchical feasts of officialdom, carnival is characterized by strange feasts, attended by oddly-matched dining companions, and celebrated in the presence of grotesque elements. Again, the central part of Kings has many examples. Ben-Hadad, king of Aram, drinks himself into incoherence (1 Kgs 20.12, 16, 18); men eat poisoned stew (2 Kgs 4.38–41); hostile warriors are unexpectedly feasted (2 Kgs 6.22–23); donkeys' heads and doves' dung are eaten (2 Kgs 6.25) followed by cannibalism (vv 28–29); there is an illicit midnight feast (2 Kgs 7.8); Jehu feasts inside while dogs eat Jezebel's body just below the window (2 Kgs 9.33–37). Each of these feasts is in some way unexpected, because it is at an inappropriate (or surprising) time, has an inappropriate menu or includes inappropriate company.

Unusual Expression of Things that are Vulgar, Grotesque or Offensive

There are plenty of instances which fall into this category, which includes elements of the grotesque, the scatological and the gruesome.

2 Kings 9 and 10 alone has several florid examples. Jezebel's body turns to dung on the plot at Jezreel (9.37), her blood spatters the walls like urine (9.33, compare v 8); seventy heads in baskets (10.7); the Baal priests are murdered still in their festal robes (10.22–25); the temple of Baal is befouled with excrement (10.27).

In fact, the central section of Kings has an exceptionally high body count, and many of these deaths are described in gruesome detail, or take place in gruesome ways. There are burnings, beheadings, cannibalism, human sacrifice, animal mauling, crushings, mutilations and a stoning. It rather reads like a murderers' source book, with enough carnage to rival even Rabelais. There is blood by the bathload; it is at times hyperbolic and bizarre in scope and intensity.[16]

Bizarre, Unexpected Breaches of Normal Cause and Consequence

Bakhtin uses the word 'fantasticality' to describe moments when there is 'bold and unrestrained use of the fantastic,' with complete freedom of plot and invention.[17] Identification of such things within a text where the miraculous is considered normal presents something of a challenge. However, the central portion of Kings contains a particularly florid cluster of miraculous and frankly bizarre incidents.

Many of the miracles in this central section are like no others in the Hebrew Bible. Kings contains the only incidents of the raising of the dead in the Hebrew Bible, and the translation of Elijah (2 Kings 2) and the other incident with the horses and chariots of fire (2 Kings 6) are unique (1 Kgs 17.17–24; 2 Kgs 4.18–37; 13.21). While not entirely unknown (consider Jonah and Balaam), the two occasions where an animal or animals act at the bidding of Yahweh or his prophet are striking. Elijah is fed by ravens (1 Kgs 17.1–7), and bears punish mocking boys (2 Kgs 2.23–25).

We have therefore found evidence within the central section of Kings for the following seriocomic features: unusual use of language; inversion of hierarchies, foolery and deception; strange feasts, the vulgar, grotesque and offensive; and bizarre breaches of the law of nature. Such events are rare in the remainder of Kings, but common here. Compare, for example, the account of the Josianic reform in 2 Kings 23 with the wild and reckless actions of Jehu recounted in 2 Kings 9 and 10. Or compare the bland accounts of political assassinations in the rest of Kings (for example, 1 Kgs 15.27–28; 2 Kgs 14.19) with the murders of Ahab (1 Kgs 22.34–38), Ben-Hadad (2 Kgs 8.14–15), or Jezebel (2 Kgs 9.32–37).

Further, the style of the central part of Kings differs significantly from the parts of Chronicles which relate the same events. The main place of overlap is the death of Ahab which we have considered several times as it is described in in 1 Kgs 22.29–40. However, in 2 Chron 18.28–34, the most florid elements are not present. Ahab is propped up in his chariot and dies. There is no reference to blood or dogs or prostitutes.

This provides further evidence to support the proposal that this central passage in Kings is peculiarly rich in odd elements, which, I have argued here, amount to a literary carnival. We will consider the purpose of this carnival in the next two chapters.

4

Satire Against Prophets

We have seen that the central part of Kings contains a cluster of carnivalesque elements. What purpose are these serving? I shall argue that, far from being represented as unerring bearers of the divine word, the prophets play a far more ambiguous role in this text. They introduce a sort of playful riot, a rumbustious revelry to the narrative. It is they who present several of the insults found within the text (as at 1 Kgs 18.27; 21.20; 2 Kgs 3.13–14), and whose dramatic revelry strikes such a contrast with the stiff pomp of, for example, Solomon. It is they who introduce the fantastical element to the text, turning the world into one where events are unpredictable, where the dead do not stay put and the living might be consumed by fire. Noting all of this may help us address one of the questions raised in chapter one: were the prophets righteous?

This chapter will focus on Elijah and Elisha, but we should note in passing that the prophets of Baal (1 Kings 18) and the false prophets of Yahweh (1 Kgs 22.1–40) are brutally humiliated by the text. But—unexpectedly, perhaps—we will discover that both Elijah and particularly Elisha are also satirized quite intensely.

Both Elijah and Elisha are also satirized quite intensely

It is worth pausing for a moment to comment on one of the essential techniques of reading biblical narrative. The author leaves clues within the text to help us to understand how to interpret the events he is narrating. Some of the most important ones relate to characterization and speech. How do people speak? What do their words reveal about themselves? Do they accurately reflect the events that the text has described? Paying attention to these details unlocks quite a lot of narratorial comment.

First we will consider Elijah, beginning with that moment on Mount Horeb (1 Kings 19) where he suffers from what is generally described as post-climactic exhaustion after his confrontation with the prophets of Baal. Elijah is generally very responsive to the word of the Lord. God commands, and he goes (as at 1 Kgs 17.3–5, 9–10; 18.1–2). But here he is found on Mount Horeb, not because of the word of the Lord, but because of the word of Jezebel (19.2). When the word of the Lord does come to him, it pointedly asks, 'What are you doing here, Elijah?' (v 9). He appears to have acted autonomously.

In fact, Elijah's actions leading up to this moment may not be as exemplary as we tend to imagine. His opening words (17.1) sound rather arrogant:

> By the living Yahweh, the God of Israel before whom I stand, there will not be dew or rain these years except at my word.

There is a subtle implication that he is arrogating to himself power over the weather. Indeed, some of the earliest commentators of this text, the medieval rabbis, express discomfort at this.[18] And following this declaration of drought, the remainder of the chapter appears to portray God working to preserve life in spite of Elijah's pronouncement; indeed, even Elijah seems to lack sustenance.

And with our reading perhaps sensitized by these suggestions of hubris, we may read Elijah's swagger on Mount Carmel as ambiguous. The text does not tell us, for example, that God ever commands the extravagant display with the water (vv 33–35). And Elijah's self-reference is quite pronounced:

> I remain a prophet of Yahweh, I alone…come near to me…let it be known that you are God in Israel and I am your servant (vv 22, 30, 36).

But if doubts have begun to whisper when we read of Elijah, they should be shouting loudly when we turn to his successor. We will briefly consider some of the elements that cause us to look askance at this man of God.

First, Elisha is far more autonomous than Elijah. Where Elijah generally moves according to the word of Yahweh, and only then, Elisha is never shown doing this. On his own initiative he goes to the bank of the Jordan (2 Kgs 2.13), to Jericho (v 28), to Bethel (v 23), to Carmel and Samaria (v 25), to Shunem (4.8), to Gilgal (4.38), into Dothan and then out of it (6.13–15) and to Damascus (8.7).

Further, when Elijah performs his miracles, they are always done with explicit reference to God (as in 1 Kgs 17.14). By contrast, in the Elisha narratives God is neither invoked nor credited for six of his thirteen miracles: the miracle of oil (4.1–7); the miraculous birth (4.15); the healing of the stew (4.41); the healing of Naaman (5.10); Gehazi's leprosy (5.25–27); the floating of the axe head (6.6–7). Two of the miracles are more troubling yet, for the prophet first attempts the miracle through his own power, and only then invokes the power of God (2 Kgs 2.14; 4.29–35). In fact, the Elisha narratives refer far more often to the word of the prophet (seven occasions, 2 Kgs 2.22; 4.17; 5.13, 14; 6.18; 7.17; 8.2) than the word of the Lord (four, 2 Kgs 3.12; 4.44; 7.1, 16). Most unsettling of all is 2 Kgs 6.18, where God is portrayed as acting at Elisha's instruction.

> So [Yahweh] struck them with blindness according to the word of Elisha.

Elisha's reputation is extensive. The Shunammite talks her husband into providing a permanent guest room for him (2 Kings 4.9) and later prostrates herself at his feet (v 37). The officials of Jericho send a delegation asking for his help (2.19). His disciples are barely able to make a move without his permission (4.1–2, 40, 43; 6.3, 5).[19] He is spoken of with awe in the enemy state of Aram, both at the royal court (6.12; 8.8), and in private dwellings (5.3). Within state life, he is at times consulted by the king with respect (6.21), and at other times held responsible for national disaster (6.31). And Elisha's own concern for his reputation is revealed in 2 Kgs 5.8 when he sends a reply to the king of Israel, who is distressed at Naaman's request for healing:

> Let him come to me, and he will learn that there is a prophet in Israel!

We touched briefly in the previous chapter on three instances where Elisha is untruthful. To recapitulate, they are:

- 2 Kgs 3.15–19 compare v 27: The partially fulfilled prophecy;
- 6.19: Elisha lies to, and tricks, the blinded soldiers of Aram;
- 8.10, 14: Elisha sends a false prophecy to Ben-Hadad and incites Hazael to his murder.

Should we conclude that Elisha is less than honest, or that he is unable to discern the word of God clearly?

One of the principal questions which might be asked of the Elisha character, then, is this: what does he *achieve*? What is the purpose of the miracle of the axe head? If the narrative indicated that Elisha gave the glory to God, we might be reassured. But he does not. Despite the fact that he is commissioned with the express purpose of eradicating Baalism, he is nowhere shown to perform this function (1 Kgs 19.17). Nor does he challenge Jezebel, arch-rival of Elijah.

Moreover, his actions are ethically dubious at times. The classic example of this is the dreadful incident with the bears (2 Kgs 2.23–25). This is one of four places in the Hebrew Bible where animals function miraculously to reveal prophets caught up in their own petty concerns.[20] However, most commentators, while expressing some discomfort about the magnitude of the response, see this story as an endorsement of Elisha's fledgling ministry. But if this is so, it is an ironic one. Elisha is being damned with faint praise: 'and *this* is how great he was!' Reading with attention to subtle subversion and critique allows us to view this story as critique, not endorsement. If Elisha appears to be acting like a bad-tempered man, that is because that is exactly what he is.

The narratives of Elisha have many carnivalesque features. He is responsible for some rather grotesque deaths and for some strange feasts; he speaks in a northern dialect; his miracles transgress the law of nature, sometimes for no clearly defined purpose; his narratives contain instances of verbal abuse, directed both towards and away from him; and they contain a number of hierarchical reversals. Throughout, the text hints that we should view him with ambivalence.

In fact, neither Elisha nor Elijah is unambiguous; neither is good or bad; both are men of God, but flawed. The carnival does not establish a new *status quo*, but rather it disrupts everything with 'joyful relativity.'[21]

We conclude that no-one is exempt from laughter. These texts serve to undermine our respect for the pompous absolutism of the prophet, be he true man of God or false prophet of Baal. They will not permit us to elevate any prophet above contradiction or mockery. He is fallible, flawed and sometimes downright ludicrous.

5 Subversive Critique of Israel and Judah

So far, we have addressed one of the three puzzles presented by the Book of Kings, as set out in chapter one. Two more remain. Why is Elijah commanded to anoint Elisha, Hazael and Jehu in 1 Kgs 19.15–17? And why are Aram and Israel so prominent in this Judean text? In order to address these questions we need to notice a further literary device within the text: the literary mirror.

Literary Mirroring

The literary mirror was described by Lucien Dällenbach in 1977. The concept derives from the heraldic device of a shield which contains a miniature representation of itself.[22] If you are familiar with Shakespeare's play *Hamlet* then you will have encountered this. At a key moment in the drama a group of strolling players present a play to the royal court. This 'play within a play'contains a mini-version of the plot of the larger play.

The literary mirror functions to comment upon the main narrative; it forms a sort of internal commentary. Sometimes it has a satirical function. We can identify literary mirroring when we detect repeated portions of text, similarity of names or repetition of circumstances.

The Command to Elijah

The central portion of Kings contains a complex arrangement of mirroring devices, which work in conjunction with its carnivalesque features to subvert and surprise. Key to this is 1 Kgs 19.15–17, where Elijah is commanded to anoint Elisha, Jehu (king of Israel) and Hazael (king of Aram). This serves several important literary functions.

When these words are spoken, Elisha is a nobody ploughing an obscure field, and both Ben-Hadad and Ahab are secure upon their thrones of Aram and Israel respectively. There is no other hint within the text that either dynasty is about to be disrupted. However, whereas Elisha is introduced in the next verse, Jehu and Hazael are still some chapters away from making their debut. These verses, then, function like a spoiler within the plot. All three men come to their new positions in striking ways. Hazael and Jehu will seize power in a series of bold, carnivalesque moves; Elisha will have power thrust upon him by an unprecedented supernatural event. These amount to three 'crowning' events as Bakhtin would understand them. It is also striking that all three men die within close proximity to one another in the text. Elisha and Hazael die in almost consecutive verses of 2 Kings 13 (vv 20, 24), and the accession of Jehu's son is in verse 1 of that chapter.

Aram makes a cameo appearance a few times in the early part of Kings, but it is not until after these verses that the nation becomes a player in its own right, with several expanded narratives. We meet the Aramean commander Naaman and his household (2 Kgs 5.1–3); we listen to Aramean court discussions about Elisha (6.8–13); and we meet the drunken king of Aram who cannot command his troops (20.16–18). So 1 Kgs 19.15–17 also appears to function to herald the arrival of Aram into the story.

These verses then, crown three unexpected leaders; they open a literary frame within which the leaders will act (and within which there is an enormous amount of carnivalizeque activity); and they unexpectedly foreground the pagan nation of Aram. This last point links 1 Kgs 19.15–17 to the third of our unresolved questions.

Mirroring of Aram and Israel

This unexpected coupling of the anointing of Hazael and Jehu indicates that a literary mirror is being established between Aram and Israel. Elijah is commanded to anoint the two kings in identical terms, and Elisha plays a similar role in precipitating both accessions (2 Kgs 8.7–13; 9.1–13). Both Hazael and Jehu are trusted by their masters: (8.8; 9.4, 15). Both ousted kings are ill at the time of their assassination (8.7; 9.15). Both new kings express initial reticence about their appointment (8.13; 9.11), but rapidly become murderous (8.15; 9.20).

There are two further key texts where Israel mirrors Aram. We will consider one in detail (the second is 2 Kgs 6.8–7.20). In 1 Kings 20 we read of a battle between the nations, where the similarity between them is emphasized. There are two kings, two armies, two nations, and two sets of counsellors; we are told twice that the two armies are camped *opposite* one another (vv 27–29). We are party to the war cabinet conversations of both kings; we watch them both mustering their troops for battle. At the conclusion of the first battle, 'Man killed his man / and Aram fled and Israel pursued' (v 20); the parallelism suggests an element of correspondence between the armies.

There are four paired conversations between the kings, which move the plot forward and develop their characters (vv 3–4; 5–6, 9; 10–11; 34). The king of Israel is shown to be prudent and God-fearing; the king of Aram is satirized as overweening, drunken and does not fear the Lord. The nation of Israel is subservient and weak but gains the victory; the army of Aram 'fills the country' but is defeated. There is a direct reversal of their situations:

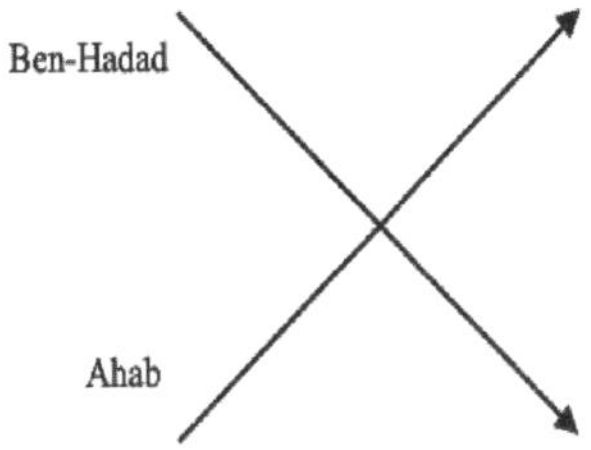

But there is a twist in the tail. The defeated Ben-Hadad sends his servants, penitentially dressed, to beg for the sparing of his life (v 32). Ahab has mercy on him, naming him as his 'brother'—another sign of literary pairing (vv 33–34). And Ben-Hadad's words, too, show a restoration of the symmetry between the nations:

> The cities which my father took from your father, I will return. And you [can] put bazaars for yourself in Damascus as my father did in Samaria. (v 34)

It is the role of an unnamed prophet to use foolery to unmask the actions of Ahab as an act of military rashness and theological arrogance (vv 35–43). The fortunes and characters of Ben-Hadad and Ahab are reversing again.

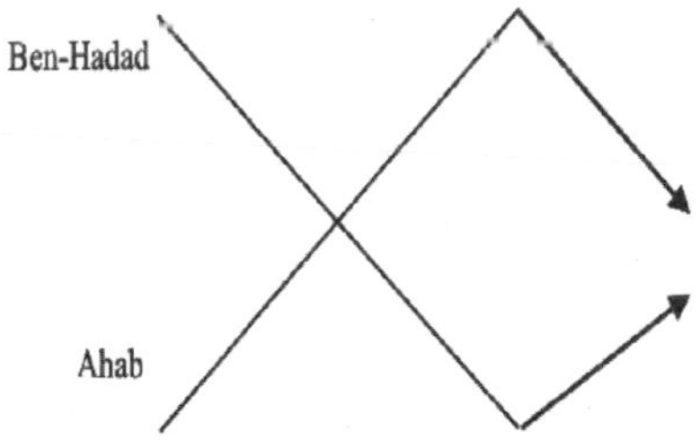

In fact, the literary pairing is even more complex. When 'Each man struck his man' (v 20), the text makes no distinction between the nations; 'in the moment of battle the sides are indistinguishable.'[23] This is then echoed in the conversation between the two kings after the second battle (v 34). When Ben-Hadad concedes the cities and bazaars to Ahab, most translations read 'Ben-Hadad said to him,' but the Hebrew only uses pronouns, (he said to him). Who is speaking becomes clear shortly, but initially some doubt is raised in the reader's mind. In response Ahab agrees to make a covenant with Ben-Hadad, but again the text leaves us in some initial doubt about who is acting, simply reading '*He* made a covenant with *him.*'

Perhaps the most telling phrase of all comes from the prophet. Ahab is told (v 42) that his life and his people are forfeit in exchange for Ben-Hadad's, 'Your life in the place of [*tahat*] his life, your people in the place of [*tahat*] his people.' The word *tahat* carries the clear implication of like-for-like substitution (see Exod 21.23 and Lev 24.18). In other words, distinct though Ahab may like to believe his actions and attitudes have been, he is so closely identified with Ben-Hadad that he is subject to the same judgment and the nations stand subject to identical fates.

The role of the literary mirror is becoming clear. The author has set up the nation of Aram as a foil to Israel, pairing speeches, characters and narrative scenes to portray Aram as the unwise, ungodly counterpart to Israel. However, once the author has tricked us into believing that this a simple comparison of good Israel with bad Aram, and to passing judgment on the evil nation, he suddenly, like the prophet (v 40), whisks the mask off and declares, as it were, 'You [Israel] are that nation!'[24]

Mirroring of Israel and Judah

This may go some way towards explaining the purpose of Aram within the text. But it does not yet explain the prominence of Israel. Why should the northern kingdom, long vanished into Assyrian exile at the time that the final version of Kings was written, be so prominent? In order to understand this, we need to notice a further literary mirror: between Israel and Judah. This is evident in many places in Kings, including a number of similarities between the story of Ahab and elements in the reigns of the Judean kings.[25] Within the central, carnivalized, section of Kings there are four key indicators.

First, Ahab's bloodline is terminated in the northern kingdom by the bloody purge of Jehu, with the apparent extermination of the whole family (2 Kgs 10.1–14). But meanwhile, in the southern kingdom, Ahab's kinswoman Athaliah becomes queen of Judah, and thenceforth, all the kings of Judah have their blood 'tainted' with the blood of Ahab's house.[26] This means that the judgment on Ahab, pertaining to all his descendants (1 Kgs 21.21–22), becomes applied to the house of Judah.

Second, this Athaliah queen of Judah closely parallels Jezebel, queen of Israel: they are both foreign queens and Baal worshippers. Many of the points of similarity between the women are communicated through carnivalized features of the text, such as inversion, the grotesque and the scatological. Both are women of violence struck down by their own subjects, their deaths preceded by strident words of defiance; both are violently slain outside their palaces, trampled by horses; and both deaths are followed by a purge of Baalism in the land.[27]

Third, King David is generally used as the touchstone of orthodoxy for the kings of Judah, who are positively or negatively compared with him (see 1 Kgs 15.3, 11). This pattern is broken in only two places, where—surprisingly—Ahab (of Israel) is used as a comparator for the kings of Judah. First, Jehoram of Judah is likened to Ahab (2 Kgs 8.18). Secondly, Manasseh, the king who led Judah into worse idolatry than the nations around them, and whose sin directly resulted in the Babylonian exile is compared to Ahab (2 Kgs 21.3), and the nations' judgments are compared: [28]

> I will stretch out over Jerusalem the measuring line of Samaria and the plumb-line of the house of Ahab. (v 13)

Fourthly, while travelling in Aram, Ahaz the king of Judah notices an altar which takes his fancy. He sends a copy of its design back to Jerusalem with instructions that it be copied and used in the temple (2 Kings 16). So we see the king of Judah being seduced by the pagan religion of Aram.

We have found a complex web of symmetries, pairs, mirrors and parallels between the nations of Aram, Israel and Judah. If the text has invited its Judean readers to see the folly and sin of Israel by unexpected comparison with the pagan nation of Aram, it twists once again, as Judah is revealed to share Israel's blood, folly and judgment.

6

Conclusion

This book has set out some novel, perhaps daring, propositions. It has argued that elements in the Book of Kings deliberately set out to mock and ridicule prophets. It has suggested that there are plot devices which invite us to laugh at kings and their actions. It has pointed out the vulgarity and the coarseness of parts of the biblical text. In this concluding chapter this proposal will be tested, briefly, against the criteria set out earlier, and some wider conclusions drawn in relation to how we read biblical narrative.

Applying the Test Criteria

In chapter two I proposed that the carnivalization of a biblical text can be regarded as proven where four conditions are satisfied. First, the distinctive features are present, and in clusters, not sporadically; secondly, the new interpretation which arises can help account for some otherwise inexplicable problems within the text; thirdly, the new interpretation should demonstrate coherence with the wider text in terms of effect; and fourthly, it should be supported by the findings of other scholars.

With regard to the first two of these: we have found distinctive features clustered in the central section of Kings; we have used this hermeneutic to provide suggested answers to the three questions identified in chapter one.[29]

The question of coherence is complex. The Book of Kings is widely regarded as having a mainly Judaean focus of interest, being highly critical of the northern kingdom's infidelity and cultic deviance, and providing a theodicy for the exiles of both nations. By its very nature, the identification of a thread of subversion within a text will unsay something that the main thread of the text is saying. Thus, if my reading were entirely consistent with the prevailing theology of Kings, it could not be satirical. Nonetheless, the use of mirroring and carnivalization to critique Israel and Judah is broadly aligned with this overall purpose.

With regard to the fourth criterion: many elements of my proposal here align with, and are built upon, the work of other scholars. In particular, parts of the satire against the prophets have been described by Wesley Bergen, and the carnivalized nature of 2 Kings 9 and 10 by Francisco García-Treto. There are, however, many original elements presented here and in the fuller publication of this research: the incidents of insults and unusual speech patterns; the cumulative weight of the violent deaths; the fools and liars within the text, and most of the unexpected feasts. The role of Aram has not even been questioned in any literature I have read. The mirroring effect between the three nations—Aram, Israel and Judah—is also a new finding, as is the way in which the text inverts at the end of the two main Aram narratives to turn the criticism upon Israel instead. Why have all of these not been previously identified? The overlooking of these themes probably has several causes. Both traditionally devout readers and higher-critical reductionist readers tend to neglect the possibility of subversion or humour. It is the comparatively recent emergence of literary criticism (by no means incompatible with a faithful, even evangelical, approach to the Bible), which has permitted some of these nuances to emerge. And, as we discussed in chapter two, a degree of deliberate concealment is to be expected in literature of this type. Certain critiques are too dangerous to express overtly.

Carnival in Kings

The world of Kings is a world of grand temples, ivory palaces and sweeping political manoeuvres. This is a world where the rich rule and the poor serve them, where the goodies are good and the baddies are bad. Into this world comes the carnival, led by Elijah and Elisha. Not for them the role of dignified elder statesman, the role of leaders of the opposition. Into the orderly, right-way-up world of Israel and Judah, they introduce a chaotic, turbulent element, a rumbustious, playful chaos, where nothing is as it seems, nothing is as you expect it to be.

In this upside-down world, brave men are found to be cowardly, men of God are revealed as egotists, enemies can become friends, and friends might stab you in the back. Here, bizarre things happen: ravens might bring you food, bears might attack unexpectedly, lions might seek you out and kill you. Here, axes float and fires break out all over the place. Here, violent death is common and might take any number of forms. You might be sacrificed by your father, beheaded with your brothers, eaten by your mother, stoned on the orders of a queen, suffocated by your servant or eaten by dogs. You can be sure there will be a great deal of blood.

This upside-down world is not a world of marble floors and ivory thrones, it is a world filled with the common stuff of everyday life, of cooking pots and oil and flour and wild herbs, of stews and bread, of lamps and beds and chairs. Here, kings might be foolish or cowardly, and prophets might fail to hear the word of God. Not in this world the grandiose speeches of the statesman or professional prayer-smith. Here, people moan and grumble, exaggerate and whine, curse and take oaths. Here, anything might happen—and it probably will. In this world, little is certain, few can be trusted, and no-one—peasant, king or prophet—is without fault or folly.[30]

Lessons for Reading OT Narrative

So what might we learn which is applicable beyond this part of Kings? First, this work highlights the value of a careful, close reading of Old Testament narrative, with particular attention to elements such as characterization, speech patterns and plot structure. This literary approach to the text has been pioneered by Robert Alter and Meir Sternberg.[31] In particular, elements of the absurd and the ludicrous should not be viewed as the opportunity to prove our orthodoxy (how many unbelievable things can you believe before breakfast?) but as an invitation to think more carefully about the opinions that the writer—and thus God—is inviting us to form about the events and characters being narrated.

This brings us to the second point: this study perhaps reinforces the need to view every character within Scripture (with the obvious exception of Jesus) as flawed and subject to critique. We should not attempt to defend the morally indefensible simply because it has been conducted by someone described as a 'man of God.' We apply this principle inconsistently, in my view. For example, most preachers are content to criticize David's adultery and murder, but many seem reluctant to call out Samson or Jephthah for their equally dreadful actions. Perhaps this is because the text overtly judges David, whereas the criticism of Samson and Jephthah is more concealed. Discovery of these covert criticisms can be difficult and time-consuming, but a good start is to approach every character with a healthy dose of scepticism.

History-telling is always a subjective enterprise

The word scepticism may make some readers uncomfortable, but I did not say we should approach *Scripture* with scepticism; I suggested we approach *biblical characters* with scepticism. But in order to allay fears that I am writing from a less than orthodox stance on Scripture, it might be in order to make some remarks about how the biblical narrative relates to underlying events.

It is a truth of the modern discipline of historical study that history-telling is always a subjective enterprise. Every account of events is limited and from a particular perspective. A history-writer will not know everything there is to know about a situation; they will have to begin the investigation of causes of an event at some specific point in the timeline, and will also have to end the analysis of its effects at a specific point. And their writing will be subjective. There is no such thing as objectivity—a story will always be told in a particular way. This is the nature of history writing and always has been. The value of it is not diminished by this reality. Most of these factors are equally true for a text we believe to be inspired by God. The comment about omniscience needs revision; the biblical historian does tell us what he could not directly know (for example, by secret conversations in bedrooms), and it is fair to assume that this is part of the storyteller's art, and is directed by the Spirit who knows all things. However, the comment about subjectivity is even more true. Consider the words of the writer of the fourth gospel, 'These things have been written *that you might believe*' (John 20.31). The Old Testament is no less purposeful.[32] It is not attempting to offer a dispassionate account of events; the ancient writer would have no interest in providing this, nor the ancient reader in reading it. It is written in order to communicate something huge and pressing about who God is, how he relates to his people, and what he is doing in the world. And the writer uses every possible strategy open to him to do it. This is not saying that the historical narratives have no connection with underlying events. It is saying that they seek to interpret those events to us, to tell us what they mean and show us why they matter.

I have no doubt that these kings were real kings and these prophets were real prophets, and that the writers are interpreting them to us in the artistic way that they write. They use as many literary devices and techniques as modern authors do. Far from being primitive and naïve, these ancient writers are skilful, subtle communicators, who have no problem in using satire, hyperbole or plot twists to help their readers to understand how we should view the characters and events they are telling us about. We must take care to read them with the subtlety they deserve.

Notes

1 The fuller version of this work is published in H Paynter, *Reduced Laughter: Seriocomic Features and Their Functions in the Book of Kings* (Leiden: Brill, 2016).
2 Translations are the author's own.
3 M Bakhtin, *Rabelais and His World*, H Iswolsky (trans) (Bloomington: Indiana University Press, 1984).
4 Billingsgate is coarsely abusive language—the language of the fishwives at Billingsgate market in London.
5 M Bakhtin, *Problems of Dostoevsky's Poetics*, C Emerson (trans) (Manchester University Press, 1984) pp 122–124.
6 In addition to the work of M Bakhtin (*Rabelais and his World; Problems of Dostoevsky's Poetics*), see also E Kirk, *Menippean Satire: An Annotated Catalogue of Texts and Criticism* (New York: Garland Publishing, 1980); P Stallybrass, '"Drunk with the cup of liberty": Robin Hood, the Carnivalesque, and the Rhetoric of Violence in Early Modern England,' *Semiotica* 54 (1985) pp 113–145.
7 W Hazlitt, 'Lecture 1: On Wit and Wisdom' in *Lectures on the English Comic Writers* (Edinburgh: Ballantyne, Hanson and Co, 1841) p 19.
8 R de Sousa, 'When is it Wrong to Laugh?' in J Morreall (ed), *The Philosophy of Laughter and Humour* (Albany: State University of New York Press, 1987) p 246.

9 M Jackson, *Comedy and Feminist Interpretation of the Hebrew Bible: A Subversive Collaboration* (Oxford University Press, 2012).
10 H Paynter, 'Ahab: Heedless Father, Sullen Son: Humour and Intertextuality in 1 Kings 21.' *JSOT* 41(2017) pp 451–474.
11 D Carr, *The Formation of the Hebrew Bible: A New Reconstruction* (Oxford University Press, 2011).
12 J Scott, *Domination and the Arts of Resistance: Hidden Transcripts* (New Haven, CT: Yale University Press, 1990).
13 Y Amit, *Hidden Polemics in Biblical Narrative,* J Chipman (trans), (Leiden: Brill, 2000).
14 These are surveyed in my book *Reduced Laughter.* The work on Kings by Francisco García-Treto deserves particular mention, as I build upon his work in constructing my own, broader, argument. (F García-Treto, 'The Fall of the House: A Carnivalesque Reading of 2 Kings 9 and 10,' *JSOT* 46 (1990) pp 47-65.)
15 M Jackson, *Comedy and Feminist Interpretation of the Hebrew Bible: A Subversive Collaboration* (Oxford University Press, 2012): P Lauter, *Theories of Comedy* (Garden City: Anchor Books, 1964).
16 For example, the 100,000 foot soldiers slaughtered and the 27,000 crushed by a wall in 1 Kgs 20.29–30.
17 Bakhtin *Problems of Dostoevsky's Poetics, op cit,* p 114.
18 Redak, quoted in R Hochberg and A Rosenberg (eds) *The Book of Kings I: A New English Translation of the Text, Rashi and a Commentary Digest* (New York: Judaica Press, 1991).
19 W Bergen, *Elisha and the End of Prophetism* (Sheffield: Sheffield Academic Press, 1999) p 176.
20 The others are Balaam (Num 22.21–35), the lying prophet (1 Kings 13), and Jonah. See D Marcus, *From Balaam to Jonah: Anti-prophetic Satire in the Hebrew Bible* (Atlanta, GA: Scholar's Press, 1995) p 168.
21 Bakhtin, *Problems of Dostoevsky's Poetics, op cit,* pp 122–24.
22 L Dällenbach, *Le Récit Spéculaire* (Paris: Éditions du Seuil, 1977) p 17.
23 J Walsh, *1 Kings. Berit Olam Commentary* (Collegeville, MN: Liturgical Press, 1996) p 301.
24 *Cf* 2 Sam 12.7.
25 For example, Ahab's coveting and appropriation of his neighbour's vineyard, and David's coveting and appropriation of his neighbour's wife.
26 M Sweeney, *I & II Kings: A Commentary* (London: Westminster John Knox Press, 2007) p 12.
27 R Branch, 'Athaliah, a treacherous queen: A careful analysis of her story in 2 Kings 11 and 2 Chronicles 22.10–23.21,' *die Skriflig* 38(2004 vol 4): 537–559.
28 This pattern is pointed out by Francesco García-Treto in 'The Fall of the House.'
29 According to the tally I have performed, there are 107 carnivalized features found between the beginning of 1 Kings 16 and the end of 2 Kings 13. I estimate that a maximum of fourteen are found in the remainder of the book. See Paynter, *Reduced Laughter, op cit,* p 120.
30 This 'Carnival in Kings' section is a quotation from H Paynter *Reduced Laughter, op cit,* p 202.
31 R Alter, *The Art of Biblical Narrative* (New York: Basic Books, 1981); M Sternberg, *The Poetics of Biblical Narrative: Ideological Literature and the Drama of Reading* (Bloomington, IN: Indiana University Press, 1985).
32 A helpful discussion of this question can be found in S McKenzie, 'Historiography, Old Testament' in B Arnold and H Williamson (eds), *Dictionary of the Old Testament: Historical Books* (Downers Grove, IL: InterVarsity Press, 2005) pp 118–425.